MEANING A CLOUD

MEANING
A CLOUD

J. W. Marshall

JW Marshall

For Lou,
with thanks
and respect
and fondness too!

my best,

Oberlin College Press
Oberlin, Ohio

Poems from *Meaning a Cloud*, sometimes in earlier versions, have appeared in *Beloit Poetry Journal*, *Cranky*, *FIELD*, *Filter*, *Golden Handcuffs Review*, *Knock*, *LitRag*, *Point No Point*, *Talisman*, and a Wood Works (Seattle) broadside.

The poems in the sections titled *Blue Mouth* and *Taken With*, with some changes, deletions, and additions, were published as letterset chapbooks under those same titles by Wood Works (Seattle) in 2001 and 2005, respectively.

From among the many deserving thanks, particular thanks for education and support go out to Nelson Bentley, Christine Deavel, Paul Hunter, Bill Knott, and the families Deavel, Marshall, Mishalani, and Sutherland.

The epigraph to *Taken With* is from Allen Grossman's poem "Of the Great House."

The FIELD Poetry Series, vol. 21
Oberlin College Press, 50 N. Professor Street, Oberlin, OH 44074
www.oberlin.edu/ocpress

Cover photograph: "Pulp ponds," © Mark Abrahamson, 1993.
Reproduced by permission.

Cover and book design: Steve Farkas

Library of Congress Cataloging-in-Publication Data

Marshall, J. W. (John W.), 1952-
 Meaning a cloud / J. W. Marshall.
  p. cm. — (The Field poetry series ; v. 21)
 ISBN 978-0-932440-32-7 (pbk. : alk. paper)
 I. Title
 PS3613.A7735M43 2008
 811'.6—dc22
                              2007041896

Contents

3. Taken With

1. Blue Mouth

Harborview Medical Center

There was this hospital
that came into my life
at the end of an ambulance.

A surge of people in a cloud
in a pool of watery uniforms
guided me through open doors.

I sank under gnat-thick language.
This was welcome to Harborview
which was thorough when I was not.

Pocket History of What Happened

I was
hit by a car
is easy to say.

Then was gotten up
onto a table
where help commenced.

When I look down
and see
years have gone.

       *

The car at the time
was everything perfection had
to offer—

German
snowflake colored
worldly—

and the day
was an unopened envelope
of snow. Radios

wouldn't leave
its contents quiet.
The problem of the future

is that we talk about it.
I was hit by a car
which lost control

in anticipation of snow.
The past is
that way too.

*

A car is an element
to transport us
through elements. Overcoat and

deliverer that
friction weather time
and our decisions undo.

I was employed
to gas cars and keep them
rolling. I got hit

and turned into a cloud come down
staining concrete
with my blue mouth going on.

*

An ambulance siren
is beside the point
like a fork beside a slice of cake.

That all-important. I was lifted
and everything went
yellow. So

yellow it beat the sky.
I burned away
but stuck around.

*

Some things are easy to say
and others take
teeth.

Once I was set onto a table
from which it is taking
a lifetime to get down.

My Confusion

I confused a stream
with life. And I confused leaves
oiling along on it
with lives. And the lake
it muscled into
I confused with a hospital's
shimmering glass doors. There was quiet
and muffled non-quiet.
And I was confused
with where exactly it was
I was going
when I heard that ambulance
moving like a mechanical leaf
through traffic.

Medic One

My saviors
          (because air must circulate)
      cut my clothing off—

No attachments.

Ghazal of the Scalpel

The day might begin or end in surgery;
that's not all that might begin or end in surgery.

Children are curious and it's curious how they learn—
imagine sex education by pretending surgery.

The hallway is a study in gray placelessness;
light pours through doors opened in surgery.

If life is the goal, and why wouldn't it be,
you can score in bed and defend in surgery.

Some knock-off of the River Styx is introduced—
the river channeled to a drip descends in surgery.

In church it's said we have a friend in Jesus,
in hospital we have a friend in surgery.

The body is so much akin to bread dough
you're a loaf, Marshall, leavened in surgery.

Shampoo & Sponge Bath

1.

It takes a small face
to see itself
in the handmirror offered

when staff says
it's time to wash that greasy hair.
Says it'll help.

Like a tuber on the pillow
or the shadow of a spade
is how

I remember looking. Water slopped
on my gown and skin and sheets.
When they laid my head back

into the metal basin
I died and happily that time.

2.

There was a terrifyingly large sky
that first day they rolled me
out for air.

Terrifyingly.
And clouds like balled-up cobwebs.
What if the chair got caught

in a crack or on a rock—I watched for that.
There's one the orderly said
meaning a cloud

that looks like you.
There was weakness in each of them.
There was a fraying wind. A mess

he said like you
before your bath.

Three Things About Walking Again

The first place after bed
is the chair—
lightpole colored chair about two feet away.
There and back
a couple maybe three times
being like a stump in a river
that makes its way downstream
rocking side to side.

The room is too much about you.
Items and gadgets have
a name taped to them
and it is yours. And who comes in
comes in for you. What killed the cat
was not the cat. Certainly
you should walk outside
and see if you can find that out.

One step then another then
the third. The stopping at the door step
where some floor is a success.
Go looking from slippers
to the push of faces and to
happened sound and
to doors and walls and elevators
and all that else. That else!

Jigsaw in the Hospital Dayroom

1.

They'd get me up to walk the floor
to the room with a world in pieces.

They might as well have spilled a box of keys;
nothing seemed to lock anymore.

No doors, no clothes, not even my faithful skin
could keep the world out or in.

2.

Want to try a piece?
she asked my first time in that too lit room—
so I lifted
a bit of the sky
and leaned with it
I was that tired
on the back of an empty chair.

3.

Maybe I should have burned the box
and those cardboard pieces.
Rid of the picture
and bits of the picture
parents visitors and all of us
maybe would have talked about
fitting ashes together.

Hospital Canteen: A Travelogue

Evening sometimes meant a trip for candy.
When permitted
to leave the floor

in sky-blue drawstring cotton pants
gown as flappy as a cloud
tannish slippers and a blue plaid robe

bag of dusk-colored urine
cane and I.V. stand and greasy hair.
Take the elevator down.

Buy a little candy.

                    *

First
tip out of bed
all shoulders like a daffodil.

The carpentry of
flowers on the move.
Flimsy

flimsy flimsy
flimsy. Ready
nonetheless to leave the room.

Shift change done and done The Evening News.

                    *

It's doorjamb to corridor.
It's out into the fluorescent breeze.
It's a shiny sheet of floor a bunch of ways.

And through each blonde open door
an impulse is on view—
standing choir of get-well cards

primrose sagging in a plastic pot
cut flowers thoughtful on the window sill.
And on each bed asleep or not

a seed or fist.

*

And which are you you might well ask.
A mess I am. But
seen through the saline sack

head-high on a wheeled chrome pole
I'm wide and pleasant.
Shivering drips enter me via needle

and urine drops flop into
the purse-like bag hooked to the pocket.
Maybe I'm a series of locks

through which what was clear grows murky.

*

Staff you can forget about like fish.
Like fish in a tank.
Because

though they love you with their
questions and thermometers
when it's morning

evenings they go quiet in and out.
There are little empty castles made for sighing over
that sit on the floor of some fish tanks.

A sigh is how it often sounds.

                    *

The elevator door
is blank as a tooth. Or
a square eye slow to blink.

A statue in the city of an Indian
welcoming white men to the shore
is how the waiting feels.

Slow to blink open on
the lit crate and its purpose.
The door open leaves a gap

to trap the wheel of an I.V. stand.

                    *

Inside my skull
the brain is full inside the elevator inside
the hospital inside the

funny string of nights and on and on.
An elevator empty but for one
can be packed.

Think about it.
There is Africa in there to say the least
and the Milky Way and the infinite.

The trip for candy is some of everything.

                    *

Red numbers cross the doortop.
Back of each a light whispers
when the corresponding floor is near

and gotten to. Not big news—
more of
a kindergarten lesson—

5 4 3
2 1
B

2B.

                    *

The appointed doors open
the appointed filmy hallway
the appointed crunchy lights and peeling paint

the LAUNDRY ROOM the RECORDS ROOM
the rooms with metal doors with no plaques at all
the doors that seep metal noise

the doors that seem to tremble.
Thick ducts roll from a boiler someplace.
Out of the elevator into that

and through it to a doorless room.

                    *

They'd painted the CANTEEN walls with milk
and it went sour.
Sour in its color and furnishings—

round wobbly tables
aluminum ashtrays crimped frilly
molded yellow plastic seats on skinny legs

like ladles tipped to pour.
A DRINK machine
and an EAT machine

and stale churchy air.

                    *

Under whatever talking happens at tables
CANTEEN is
the molten core of

nothing much to do.
Like entering a light bulb
but able to breathe

and conduct commerce there.
Coins warm in the palm in the pocket.
The spark comes reaching from

thought to coin slot.

                    *

Candy hangs inside its machine
like keys in a motel office.
There are

CHOCO-PLEASE YOU bars in tangerine wrappers
WHO NEEDS NUTS??? in vacation-colored slacks
daisymilk boxes of ME 'N MY FRIEND

for instance. These and those.
And above each
a price in heavy little black numbers.

Figure what adds up to that.

                    *

In front of the candy machine is
that loneliness
voting has about it.

The equality of choice is such
one might as well go stand on a beach
without the sense of touch.

SECURITY sometimes comes in and leaves.
Whatever I pick
brings its 1.7 ounces to

the pocket weighed down by my urine bag.

              *

Going back is like studying a rubber band—
roundness pointless in itself. The wrapper
unwads in the trash like a knife fight.

And no candy lasts as long
as wondering what it really tasted like.
Then wondering so what so goddamned what.

Inside the box of being awake
is the box of being asleep and vice versa.
And inside each is a health and a dream

and a hammer and a building to break and fix.

              *

Coda:

One night
in a pain-killer sleep
I dreamt I climbed into a cedar like into a blanket.

The green became completely black
and everything else was yellow and screaming
with *day* written all over it.

Slice that
cedar shadow thin and rectangular
and wouldn't you have

a decent chocolate bar?

* *

Television in Hospital

1.

Always on
that tender fixture dressed
emptiness up
like a circular parade
seven days long with faces
changing on the hour
and the half.

My blue calendar
my blue watch
bolted to the room's white wall.

The image that has joined me until death
is of a glad dog bounding toward
its meal and the hand that left it.

2.

I'm a mirage before
the television I'm a
mirage shimmering delighted since
my show's on my show offers more
substance than
I can a mirage
shimmering in the bed
sure you can touch my toes
which gives you I guess
a certain meaning but
must you visit while
my show's on

The Nightshift Nurse Brought
Her Shoes to Work in a Paper Bag

And changed in a narrow room with a bench and a sink and her own yellow locker in a row of yellow lockers for which she supplied her own lock. Lunch and the good shoes locked away until break and then just the shoes until her going home. That someone would steal from a nurse on duty that nurses stole from nurses on duty what the hell was health care after all?

I loved her I guess because there was nothing else which is not to say I didn't really love her. Because there really was nothing else. The t.v. was nothing and the curtains that did the U around my bed were pointless really because light and noise and just anything at all got past them and because if she didn't come and talk to me didn't ask me something about me I really think I would not have existed just the furniture there. And I really did love how her professional shoes ached out loud like seagulls in the hall when she walked and that with the phone chimes sometimes and the elevator bell sometimes and sometimes my voice that needed her more that called *nurse* out to her but I know really wasn't calling her but was calling *nurse* because of how calling *nurse* felt how righteous and pathetic it felt to call *nurse* from a dark room into a lit hall. What with all that I loved the sound of her shoes the shoes she put on for work that answered me.

Sadness Therapy

On the second floor
the doors had plaques attached
to indicate the duties of their rooms.

Physical Therapy
Occupational Therapy
Chaplain and others.

Behind the Sadness Therapy door
a reproduction of Picasso's Guernica
took up most all of one wall.

And there were shelves
muddled with paper and stubby pencils
gray clay in glass jars

fringe and beads for macrame
and wood and paints and nails and glue.
Sit at that table my counselor told me

and focus on the horse's throat.
I want you to make me a model
of what you think it has to say.

I could not move.
That happens he said.
I'll take you back to your room now.

The t.v. in my room that night
played a talk show with the horse as guest.
The audience let go some laughter

while the hacked animal
tried to reassemble
in the yellow chair beside a potted palm.

I guess, the host said,
you knew Picasso extremely well.
I turned the channel

to a sports show
where they ran a clip of the horse
crumpled over a ten-foot putt

certain to rim it
and face the derision.
I switched then to the public station

where a panel discussed Picasso's Guernica.
The author of The Definitive History
of Bombing Civilians tisked and said

the death toll certainly doesn't warrant
the size of the canvas.
He said well then imagine Hiroshima.

The critic of the use of pigment
said I figure this more
as something for plastics. I'd rather be

walking among the jagged relics
than having to stand so far away.
The last panelist was The One True God

who said I'm simply perplexed
by such sympathetic treatment of
what was after all a box of beasts

that fell apart. Don't they all?
I turned the t.v. off.
There was no more need.

I'm ready to go home
I told the doctors on their morning rounds.
Have you made a model of the horse's voice?

Listen to me
I said
knowing the answer.

Bare Tree at Green Lake

Out from the hospital of it,
what they call the trunk,
comes its very stopped reach.

What they call wood, call branches,
I call leaves-asleep, call
requisite thwarts.

What they call recovery
I call the amazing nothing compound,
this gargantuan receding day.

They call this walking around the lake.
I call it I was here.
I am part of the hospital now. Even now.

2. *Where Else*

Within Limits

Our neighborhood shares
a maple's blazing red leaves
but not the firewood.

Every State Its Own Quarter

One recent aspect of
our freedom was
a contest to design a coin

The large agreeable Indian man
worked the sidewalk in
an Easy Mart's blue ice light

60s apartment buildings each side of the street
were linear and balconied like
orthodontia and a mirror

He offered a
perfectly dead and shriveled rose
banter and a loony dance

The image of a salmon and the mountain
distinguish our state's quarter
from those others

One white couple on their way out
took the rose for change with
smiles all around

The weather for the moment was
less aggressive summer than we'd been having
much to everyone's relief

Chickadee Sketches

1.

A patch of night attached to the cedar—

the thing of it is
it's a pocketful of caution

present as the crack in a cup.

2.

The chickadee bobbed
on a dead lily stalk
and was all the talk
of the cat at the window.

3.

I was
watching that chickadee in
a future life
        so
please don't feed me anything having anything
to do with
time as a linear construct.

Two Facts

Walking downtown
is like putting together a jigsaw puzzle
without any border pieces.

Watching a movie is like
putting together a jigsaw puzzle that is
nothing but border pieces.

Free Zone

Outside the trial trees were allowed
and cars were allowed and commerce was.
I'd taken the bus and downtown
is Free Zone and people are allowed to
get on and off for free. This is how
some of the difficulties of the city
get around. A wall of broadcast trucks
was shiny outside the Courthouse

their dishes extended and
anchors drifting around with scripts.
A man shot his Cambodian purchase because
she said she wanted out even though
he'd spent a stack on her and her mother.
The jury was due back. I felt
like I looked like a good apple in the seat
and I wanted to have that effect.

The city went by in dollops. And though
I have never done anything a woman
roping down the aisle pinched her teeth
and dropped all herself without a
whiff of delicacy next to me then
said out loud I don't care how much
money you have I could hurt you.
I said nothing just like any apple.

April

Reading while walking
a fist of cherry blossoms
punished her.

A Contemp Lament

Everything costs too much
so is on sale. However
the miracle of walking upon a parking lot
must not be discounted. There were
boys in a car with a
wrecking ball taking on
their speakers. A girl
talked in a window to them and
just where was her skirt?
I'm getting old. So old I read
obituaries for
hints on the personal narrative. I'd gone
to the mall in search of
a solid sweater and was
met by headless mannequins
dressed I guess
for the season's decapitation parties.
Surely somewhere
John the Revelator points to the practice of
taking an additional half off the sale price at the register
and says *See?*

Rules of Engagement

There's a one day sale
on at Macy's and though
earlier there was
gunfire on Lake City Way and
reports of gunfire at the downtown Courthouse
you're okay.
> Just remember to
say *Oh! Ouch!* if
someone means you harm.
With
conviction:
Oh!! Ouch!!

And if someone parking
> where you're parking shouts

you-drive-like-a-motherfucking old woman

> wear the shawl.

A one day sale on at Macy's
all week.
I call my Visa
The Hammer of Justice
and my MasterCard *The Bell of Freedom*
and I oh yes I
am the striking force.

Dear Hummingbird

You're not alone.
It's taking me ages
to learn the red leaf isn't a flower.

This Is a Crime Watch Neighborhood

It's lawful to walk
through this neighborhood
just like it's

lawful to page through a copy of LifeStyle
in the magazine stand at the Market while
fish stink and

junkies watch the tourists' wallets.
But this is
the neighborhood of subscribers.

And here came one
like a pair of scissors down
her pansy-ribboned path.

Tired of walking's how I replied
to her question how you doing?
Walking's good for you

she said with two meanings.
What hundred block is this
I asked as though something nearby might

be waiting for me.
Sixteen hundred she said.
Same as the century.

Then was around to her door.
Left me alone with
an eye on a phone pole.

Be legal
I heard but it could have been
somebody calling a dog.

Christine's Some Mornings

Because you woke up
it started raining.

Rain like eyelashes.

The radio asked
warfare or murder?

The dog wants her walk
is how she loves you.

Murder or warfare?

Rain like eyelashes
because you woke up.

Not Let Across the Hood Canal

Like public funded art
it is a threat

Makes the traffic stop
because
a tender's opened up the bridge

The surfaced submarine is heading out
that tendon in
the global lurk and shove

At the railing oohs and ahs

The hills around
are green as stacked green towels

Children roar to life
like tassels yes the wind
will make you okay teary

A Trident sub
is canary black is
black is solitary as a mile marker

We have everywhere to be
and have to wait

Dream Occupation

Every place there was made of stone.
Stone street and plaza.
Stone sky.

They'd come to me one by one asking
what sounded like calm hushing questions.
Questions for a baby.

Delightful music they'd ask me over and over.
But I was a soldier.
What had happened to threatening?

One brought a steaming cup of lavender tea.
One brushed my shoulders three times.
I was without back-up.

When do I fire?
This was ease for which I had no training.
Lovingly taunted. Tickled.

I think they were asking little boy
what do you do with your gun?
And laughing. Even I was laughing.

Surrender.
I kept saying I
surrender.

July 14, 2006

Any special God-awful news this morning
other than having Andy Williams's *Moon River*
looping through my head? The chickadees
were out of food so I put seed in their feeder.
It could be said I fed them but why say it?
Then newspaper.
                    What was Beirut before
slag and plumes and agony? Any
happy birds there? Why not try to
figure how to spoil your enemy? I guess
I'm simple.
                    Anyway my huckleberry friend
has left and sweet *Good-Bye Pork Pie Hat*
has moved in. Nothing less
haunted makes any sense today.
Seattle is a rubble kit too.

For the Guest Book

The accommodations were
lovely. We are sorry
this was such a
terrible time. We had all
the appointments we could
use. None failed. Thank you. We
only wish we had been
here other days. All
the faces have become
handkerchiefs. Ours too.
The sunset became a
handkerchief. A sleeve.
So sad. Even this
glorious place. Our
thanks in any case
for what was meant to
make us comfortable.

Exit Poll

Flock of robins
who did you vote for?

The Dog Sandy Lets Us Go

A blue cloud staggering to
the corner means
more adjusting of the carburetor

A small man guns
a small chainsaw that Douglas fir
has limbs lower than he likes

Kids down the block scream
gleeful oops one steals the show but
the wound is not new long

She carried this around
the busy plants and insects and birds
the raining and the snowing

Carried the neighborhood around and now
has set it down so lovingly
few even realize

Christine, Christine

If I did not love her teeth I would not stay

3. Taken With

> *There is*
> *No singing without a woman who wants*
> *An answer sufficient to her injury—*
> *Such is the muse.*
> —Allen Grossman

1.

It used to be
I'd take my mother shopping.
Took her to a grocery store

where she was known.
Hello Eleanor we'd hear.
Everybody here's

so friendly's what she'd tell me then
get behind a cart and we were off.
We'd tour the five names of apples

piled in their five bright hills.
At the banana bin she'd say
get me that one there and

get me that one off of that bunch please.
There was no losing her because
her gravity grew stronger the

smaller she got.
When I go down an aisle where
I don't find a thing to buy

it's exercise
she told me once.
Pleasantness was a whip we each

knew how to crack.
I could reach
the bonus pack of paper towels.

She'd talk herself into
a second éclair. Twos of this and that
made their way

into her wire ark. Just one more row
she said John I don't know
what they might have down there.

I went along
in tow to
her hunger and her curiosity.

2.

Phone on the wall at work it rang.

I brought it over and was told
check your mother. Was told
she's not picking up John but I know
she's there. Please would you please go and check?

I had a key.

In the corner of the kitchen she
was on the floor she's on the floor and says to me
John help me up with half her mouth
and this ought not to be.

This is no horizon to ever go and see.

Says John please help me up I don't think I should.
Help me up I'm calling 911.
Just help me up and I say no
and we go on from there.

3.

The Queen of England brought a questioning device
she held up to my mother's left ear.
Nothing to fear.
She was quite nice.
We want to know what goes on in there.
My mother smiled thinly as her hair.

She asked who was a president ago
and the color of my mother's mother's eyes.
My mother tried
and tried but no.
The Queen of England read a meter
then said Oh like in some theater.

Would you read me I asked Her Grace.
She wrote down something that needed writing down.
Her eyes were brown
and he was such a waste
my mother blurted out. The Queen said I'll let doctor know.
Mother said John when can we go?

4.

My distemper
Mother called the toothpaste foam
waiting for an aide to help her rinse.

All day long she said I'm D.I.C.
my niece the veterinarian having once told her
the code for Dead In Cage.

Not a pet exactly but now
an animal that's taken to saying thanks
for most anything at all.

5.

Like into a forest filled
all with things I didn't know
I woke into her stroke.

Her hair got rinsed
in the roommate's t.v.'s blues.
I was on the margin of her sleep.

The figure of her skull
was oh so clear. The figure of her soul
was who knows where.

Lost in those woods and sitting still
I heard a voice
that could have been the air

and it told me
she used to be your carriage now
it's up to you to come and go.

6.

In the Dining Hall a pod of women and two men were pointed toward the acting reader who had first checked their brakes. The reader took a blue book up and read the story of a hemophiliac boy with AIDS and then two broken legs from when his school bus ran him down. Still he believed in Jesus and was a darling imp at home. He died in total grace and love. You think you've got it bad and then you hear... the reader said. Joyce whose voice was like a bent clock spring said an Amen.

Mother had the Lipton tea in a thick maroon plastic mug and just one slice of the white cake thanks.

7.

I made a Tuesday visit and she was in
the Dining Hall faking hymns
one of that sock puppet chorus who'd been
cornered in faith by dour Scandinavians.
Their boom-box and large print.

I waited in her room then left a note:
who's this Christ the King you're hanging out with?
love, your bitter son John

8.

Away from her I folded into
my car in Building D's parking lot

and sat inside that trinket
ordered with others in lettered slots

then went from fraction to a whole
by backing up and driving off.

The difficulty was in how
to act the part

east-bound on 130th.

9.

George Burns was where she was—
the t.v. console end of the hall
and her there saying
                        sit right here.
An old modern comedy she
laughed at up and down
like a crow you might not want
to walk beneath.
                        I think I saw this
show before she said.
Was it you I saw it with?
I said I hope it was.
                        They
used to call me Gracie
your father did when I
was dizzy.
                        She turned sad.
I said honey I still think you are.

10.

The pool table's in
an otherwise empty third-floor room

Let's not think about the various deaths

There's a Serenity Room and a
Chapel too
on the third floor

Let's not

It's easy enough to find them—
the pool table is
in the room by the Card Room

near the Dining Room so I don't know why
the room is empty when we get there
and empty when we leave   .

11.

The library door's hard to get through
for this mother, son, and wheelchair stew
but there's a limerick book
and we each like to look
at the one that rhymes rescue with screw you.

12.

A coin minted with
Second Floor Nursing Wing on one side
would have to have
a form of suicide on the other.

Heads:
she smiled sweetly as a nectarine.

13.

The day visitors brought their pets
I rolled Mom to the patio.
Summer was losing its grip
which meant a shawl and hat for her.
We said we liked it though.

Some kid was entertained
by bringing out two gerbils
each motoring a plastic globe they
knocked around the cobblestones and
wheelchairs and families' shoes.

Mother said of them I hope they don't
find the stairs. She never liked
to go that way herself.
A silver standard poodle came
quiet up to her and set

its muzzle on her uncovered hand.
Her sigh went on in stages.
The stink of chlorine from the pool
framed the beds of tended roses.
My eyes stung for reasons.

The poodle left and Mom said
this sun's so nice I think I will
close my eyes but don't you dare
take me in. We sat there like
a garment slung across two chairs.

John she said her eyes still shut
do those roses all have names? I said
I'm sure they do. And pets have names?
Of course they do. And you and I
have names. I wonder why.

14.

At the end of Sunday Exercise they
sing Row row row your boat sing
Michael rowed the boat ashore

but mostly they sing made-up sounds
who've lost their way
who've run aground.

15.

I'd wheeled Mother where
Faith Hour was slated to begin
after the chaplain got there

wiping first her chin
because a spoon in her hand
was an inexact tool.

I was set to leave.
Where are you going Mother asked.
I'm going home.

Take me with you she said
and laughed a kind of wreck.
The woman to her left

said take me with you too
then the six or seven of them all
took the sentence on

like hail taking on a garbage can.
Take me with you haw haw haw.
Take me with you laugh laugh laugh.

Like a headache made of starlings.
I can't I said I have a wife and dog.
A dog haw haw haw haw.

A wife laugh laugh laugh.
Take me with you take me with you.
Haw haw laugh laugh laugh.

I zippered my coat closed
with a ferocity that shut them up.
Unbalanced silence in the room. Mom

knocked it over saying
you should go.
Saying I've been where you're going.

Anyway go walk your dog.

16.

No longer is she
my mother whose voice was
the voice in the whirlwind whose voice
was the voice of the burning bush
whose ear I'd always thought
bent to hear me.

17.

The elevator's walls were
copper-colored jute-like stuff
year-around. I and a couple with

a cardboard box of gifts
rode in it
nodding at each other once

as if in harness.
First floor to second floor
where we met

a string of women
chairs backed up against the wall
below a green crepe swag

hanging nowhere to nowhere.
Mother among them
said who are you? The Magi?

The couple knew
where they wanted to be
and went off that direction.

The woman on Mom's right said
we're just watching Christmas pass
like a car.

18.

They made music play
so that I might scrape my head against it
in the car.
            They made
silence so that I might
follow along
                in the car.

I didn't think about
her head like a dented pail and
her breathing
                there like
sand taken out
by the tablespoonful.
                    I didn't
think
        until the news came saying
an immense tragedy happened—

that astronauts
                lit the sky for miles.
What sky?
            The sky. For miles.

19.

She was nearly sculpture in the bed.

My wife and I at bedside found
things to say—
   mice in a cabinet find
the little left.

Supper trays were passed out down the hall.
Her chest just slightly
rose and fell
      like a plywood sheet
someone lately dropped in place.
Then that breathing slipped below
the wall clock's pick pick.

A nurse came in
   and listened and said
there's still some sound.
Said to us talk to her she's on her way
then left the room.
I leaned in against an ear
and gave her her good grades.

At last she said I've passed but we
were in an altogether different class
and could not hear a word.

Imagine how a rock becomes complete.

20.

My wife called
my sister Eleanor died called
my brother Eleanor died called
my sister Eleanor died while I
slumped in a chair like
a skein of yarn.

21.

Two-bit paper open
to the obits where
she is a clump of text among
clumps of text that make the most
boring jigsaw puzzle all because
they fit together with such ease.

Eleanor Wallace
all loss is small loss
Eleanor Wallace

22.

I was back to help clean out her room when
an old man misaligned in his wheelchair shouted
Young man come here from a corner of the lounge.

No staff visible and again Young man come here.
I went and stood in front of him like we were in the military.
Young man I have a question. I said yes?

Was that man I saw a while ago over there my mother?
I've rarely felt as certain as I did then and I said no.
He said again I want to know if that man I saw a little while ago

was my mother. No panic in his voice just level curiosity.
I said no again like I was a visiting academic. Are you certain?
I'm certain I said and he said Okay. I just wanted to know.

Thank you young man. I went back to her last room.
And what if I had said I'm your mother and still love you?

23.

Round like a hatbox
lift the lid
the world an urn and ashes.

24.

From a dark scuffle in laurel leaves
the dog produced a tennis ball
that sixth night after Mother's death.

She the dog Sandy was grand with joy
and swaggered it home
like a sailing ship to port with plunder.

Again the next two dogwalk nights she found
tennis balls along our path
and they went home with her.

I swear this was Mother's way
of saying things
had gone okay.

25.

I am beyond tired because
my mother
slipped off.
            The slow theory that
she would vanish has
come to fact.
Now she is dead all the time.

The sky is some but little
company.
           So much
simple weather which is
her having gone
pulling the scenery with her.

The industry I have left
is something like a person's who
reattaches leaves to trees
making winter summer seeming.

26.

At her house once
a hawk struck juncos she
admired out the window.
A blurring shock of

hit and then
silence the width of several yards.
She wept a pinch
and stood until a chickadee

broke the spell
nipping to the feeder and away.
A chickadee she said. Good.
I've got a sack of feed I'd hate to waste.